A Mouthful of Hardship and Honey

Alexandra Ellen Appel

First published 2024 by The Hedgehog Poetry Press

Published in the UK by
The Hedgehog Poetry Press
Coppack House, 5
Churchill Avenue
Clevedon
BS21 6QW

www.hedgehogpress.co.uk

ISBN: 978-1-913499-80-8
Copyright © Alexandra Ellen Appel 2024

9 8 7 6 5 4 3 2 1

A CIP Catalogue record for this book is available from the British Library.

for John and Brenda:

love and memories live on

CONTENTS

Thirteen Love Poems

5 for Ireland

10 Life Lessons

3 Miscellanies

13 Love Poems

(the profound stillness- where there is so much noise so much
interference)

dear dark man, man
under leaf and mold,
dark dark moon man
of the silenced house from which no secrets come
the hydra headed who, from an open door,

examines
where you sit,
infusion of flower, leaf and mold
cocoa in hand, rocking with the already dead.

When we meet again at the Crossroads
carrying our boots and baggage
shadowed with waves of light
a turn of starlings and sand birds,
remember what we did not say.

for Jesse Longacre
1952 -1993

Random Effect

For R.

behind my eyes
wanting grace
in distant
range   the hills once shared

and hills melting
as rain dishonors March,

field and hills
behind my eyes
and sun dimming
when we part

Random Effect

Inventory, for J

Venus curls
round your thighs,
my finger tips

there!
a cup of coffee, shadow and sun light lights
the kitchen table

from the garden,
mint and lavender,
a slug along the terrace wall

history created your mouth

I would be all you dream
it wouldn't be enough,

I wait for the fog to return
it's yes
all the times I want to say yes.

the last love poem, the devil's dream

in the waters of an inland sea
I held your hand in the devil's dream
how the whirlpool called us down and gulping water
took the weak her fate and I was yours
but for the tree of dreams where hangs a song

      in the innocence of all things
      among the soup spoons
      and crock pots, the potted plants,
      a golden fish
      in a bowl
      on a counter

      your hand in mine,
      the taking of the devil's claw

later, we walk the streets.
The crying frogs
call out your name,
tuly fog and dank mist
catch my breath,
suspend my hand in yours

      the rushing mist
      caught fragrant and alive

ourselves,
silhouettes walking
      claw to claw, mocking
      the devil's dream, our song
      my hand on your penis
      there was such moisture
      between us
      what can we be sure of,

I felt your breath on my bones
I felt such will of you
beneath the small shadow of myself
on the crying street of a broken highway

who killed the golden fish then,
the devil's dream? Claw by claw.

Random Effect

Sunday Morning, for J

sliding across the August sky
Sunday morning laps in
in sunny waves

history comes too
in bunches,
like yellow jackets

to the old Plum tree,
sweet rotting plums
every August, juicy

as if it weren't enough to eat this fruit and remember
our history like the fruit, as if the fruit were too much to bear
and not strong enough to take home and root

like you and I
sliding across the August sky.
If I could return to anything it would be the stars

if you could be everything
you would take our history and the yellow jackets and the August sky

and it would barely be enough
but who would care

Random Effect

When Snow Becomes Water, Not Fox

the tracks in the snow
are not from fox
the same with my imagining
you, not who you are
somehow not who I am either
which makes us equal

the tracks in the snow
are dog, not fox
this is real, different
not the same as before
when young we knew nothing

I love the imagining
the what could be
and most likely
will never

there pause
and begin again, too many lifetimes
lived in a solemn wish
to regret nothing to bend no truth
to hold the present wish full if only
the tracks in the snow

were ours, the dying afternoon
held in each others arms
the sweet angel of love
the world our hearts
our mistakes our beginnings
our end, O love.

Mountain Time

he never lived a life
of sudden occurrences the way
she has, money

is his friend, not
hers, he
has not dropped
on to concrete

in the process
shattering the remains
of past longings
leaving her

in wonder
for the present
condition
this

is.
True.

Hawk, Lost Love

our
boundary as in crossing a river
a river as in direction. I would

call you friend
any name divides us
or we have no names
only our decisions as in direction as in boundary.

I would say it this way:
A gaunt
face stares from a window
a train goes by, due north, the window
faces a river, the sun sets west. In
all directions there is the Sky.   Not
as in a sky but The Sky. And the

division becomes easy only the difference is cruel
as in direction or our story about the
eagle. It is a hawk but I want
to name it eagle.

You haunt me
hawk. As in decision
as in the difference of names

these boundaries are ours
these are our divisions
these are our
decisions

Random Effect

They say
she sleeps with the steel nose
of a gun locked
between her thighs

They say
she has teeth
where other women are soft, the
softness and color of ripe plums

But she
has teeth and sleeps with the cold steel nose of a gun locked
(steel of a gun) locked
between her thighs

and nothing can enter her now, can enter now

Random Effect

wind forces itself
through winter trees, the branches
rake against my heart

remember the wind over the plain of our beginning,
will I ever be free, your gun
sits on my desk. But it is empty.

Random Effect

These artifacts, these fetishes, what
have they to do with me, you
are of the earth and I am air
the distance between is great

how did the skull
the caribou's empty spirit
sulk their way back

I am of the air, you
are earth. The distance between us is past
why have you willed the return
what pleasure is yours in haunting me

Earth, dry bone and skull, parched
thirst you possess me
earth desert cracked barren, you
forsake me

wither bleach my bones crumble
my skin becomes dust, I am
air and you have gone too far

nothing remains
not even your shadow.

Random Effect

betrayed by my body
the lust it held besotted by a tsunami

of age related malapropisms gone the light hearted
laughter and getting some of what

ever it is,
these days the couch is refuge

keeping me from starving to death,
the small Dog I love without requirements

5 For Ireland

for John
d. June 6, 2021

On Clare Island, I've a merry devil to thank

in the rocky brambles laced on a lonely patch of heather and sheep shit
a wooly shamrock, all wet it is big as the palm of me hand
and rain, fair to say a slicker is preferred

who would argue what remains are held in blood? I suppose
ship wrecks from the western sea blow ashore, O the blow of it
a cause and a cure,

tucked inside me pocket, otherwise what use a pocket?

Pernod

drinking the emerald liquor
the green Ile herself we were

the thatched roof
received silver-lit rain

and there to the north, Benbullen
for you, then,

the liquid drops echo
on the bare wood floor

For you, then,
Thereupon,
Propped upon my two knees
I kissed a stone.

for D.H.

silver the Bay
beneath the wing

under a not-full-moon,
I was flying anyway, this time aboard Pernod

thinking of Her I have not forgotten,
Our Queen, Maeves

Will we all not flock
to Ellen's pub then

once more, the past
riddles the present

walking the high street to Christy's we were
at the half
after a cappuccino, a slice of apple pie

after a paddle in Clew Bay
a kelp strewn beach
and curious waves slapped against our ankles

a mastery of limestone and events
feeding the very bone of the earth beneath our fire

for Maggie

Prayer for My Soul

bathe me in the Irish Sea
coat my body with salt and kelp from the western shore
leave me at the Crossroad where the well runs deep

in the light of Autumn
let the falling of leaves cover me
until the geese return

10 Life Lessons

liberated into mid-morning sun
dog hurls into the river,
this and nothing more gives way from the cooling night

a feather requiring nothing, floats on the river

> 'Ridiculous, who ever heard of such a thing?'
> Mother mocks the idea of the particular nature of all
> phenomena

as if nothing is possible,
river rock, glacier rock, sea rock,
toad in my garden, wet dog

Might as well be
lost in the South China Sea we have
lost the signal from the heavens

where are we
who knows the direction,
the stars of course

the wind is jeopardy
at times the tilt of our own heart
is misleading,

return to Ecclesiastics
to Solomon who knew
wisdom has it's limitations and is not man's main concern

It is an old story
ask any woman.

for my friend Sam

In a dark time, the eye begins to see
T. Roethke

follow the boom tide moon of yesterday
into the hot reality of today

days like today I don't want to bring forth the wrong shape
there is a wrong shape, you do know

it is colored in the dark and left there for all who can not see to see
best not pick it up, walk on

carry water in cupped hands to those of us who are thirsty.
True Story. Takes after Life, no imitation

Why deny the obvious child
Paul Simon

29

let the silence seep in
find comfort in the light

the night demons
won't stay

after all
they only exist in your mind

how hard they work
to see you wake

the cold knowledge
some-thing isn't quite right

you don't have answers
who would you ask if you could,

recall Angels of Mercy Grandma brought from the old country.
Be graceful, and get on with it.

Would I want time to freeze?

Let the world be, let the fires end
Let the summer day shimmer in cascading glory
Let the peace of truce fly on wings dedicated to tolerance

Let this be the end of the beginning,
It is no small matter water flows
As if time were any less than fluid

25 April 2021

languishing, I bury my face
in the softened pelt of Mother's mink
the remnants of before now

before pandemic
before 9 minutes and 32 seconds
before wild fires

Sacred rage,
like magpies interested in the next shiny bauble
I go on

the Western Shore

and so it falls to early ruminations
paring apples for tea,
I might consider
the wind blown sea for the truth
is more than I can bear
or so it feels
best be inside the poem, there is

the hearth-
had this happened before
or so I imagine
 reading Edgar's ruminations in the Wood
          Poor Turlygod! Poor Tom!
pacing the worn oaken floor bare
except for the grim
ash driven pits
when too much spit
erupted the spirit from the fire
and all went quiet
and the sea

it is the way, with owls and spiders
so much for truth that is

because yarrow grows across the continents

in summer the wild
yarrow too reminds you there is life everywhere beyond
the shuttered blue globe of your infinitesimal bubble, look

       You, I am talking to you
       Wake the fuck up

the placement of things
is of finite import
something you should know, or

find time to find
you see, nothing is as it seems to some
while others see nothing

take the Gap for instance
it's there, a reminder
to watch where we step,

if only to do as we are told and we are, told

in the concentration of efforts
scuttling truth is a reflexive pronoun
sometimes a verb, hear the silence.

Gravity, for Mother

could it be
in dream the truth reveals
itself, for instance have I dreamed

half finished sweaters Mother knitted
jade green, the softest mohair wool
another, sky pale blue

would I keep
or toss away like bad dreams forgotten
her crystal goblets, her silver service

In another life would I want these dreams,
in this half lived life of mine lived in
boxes and storage and empty spaces

      etymologies of the rarest kind
      have no language, only swamps of imagination
      where dreams and death might justify
      the unwiring of a life
      where death is just a tiny spark of will

      how we do not live
      how we do not speak of dreams,
      the simplest truth

without our dreams
what happens to truth
to half knitted sweaters
to goblets and silver when we die?

Gravity
being the hidden weight of all things
possible.

Oughta Be A Law

there she goes
x-ing the fricken floor
the upstairs drunk
what a life. Crashbamstomp

alakazam, in a moment
the whistle of the kettle
the washing machine whoosh and strum
the dogs' soft snore
wanting, waiting, more

3 Miscellanies

THE IMPORTANCE OF WATER and ash

and, in gratitude to the light
the meticulous wish of leaf and mold, the dark green
stem of reproach and yearning
the bringer of all things,
the molecular structure of matter, a question of DNA
and belief
or, how the darkening clouds carry rain: an old wives tale
hidden among the brambles, raspberries gone wild in the tall meadow grass

      I was left, a widow with a small boy
      staring at the coldness of the Peak, holding on...
      my two draft horses hauling in the wood, the huff of breath in the frosted air,
so cold ice held
      my hands cradle the small child, the warmth
      alls' I need the long winter after the old man died. listen, the wind
      come up the north side of the slope, busting through the cabin
      and the snow, till break-up

so much water carrying the stories. delicate, blue veined, the cold trace
along the old lay lines where the spring surfaces, and becomes a bog, soft and mushy
ripe for jack-in-the-pulpit and yellow marsh-mallow, the broad stroke of solomon's
seal, a brook and then a well, where a rusted bucket waits from which we drink and
are forgiven

moss covered granite and quartz marking boundaries,
the bloom on lilac gone by from grief and abandonment and hope
rotting marsh and memory, the insult of free will
and a thousand times yes repeated to form a mantra
released to wind,

prayer flags
a simple act of faith
a bead of sweat
the long forgotten hush of our bodies
the trill of a hermit thrush in the deep wood
no less than twilight, or water, no less than ash.

erratic, limestone lowlands

there you have it
the glaciated remains
in a million years will lose the flavor
even though you have tasted the beauty
it will not be your fault, best to forget
you have thought it over
and concluded nothing remains
it is, to be honest,
the present we all forget
in accordance with the burden
of the slow evolution
of that which always will be
as if to say, life
has other meanings would no doubt
be an understatement
surviving the slow erosion
of time no matter how much
thought you have given
in the end nothing remains
except the moment, always that, the moment
the honeycombing of limestone as if
the bees are already present
leaving behind a scarp
of reverence

at the River Mist

I.
you carved
my bones from turtle, shaped a mantle
of sea salt and spray
took from bear a heart

and left me like no other
to catch a sorrow of dreams
a golden husk, the blanching of bone and shells and feathers
willed me to being

for your efforts I dance with seals
assemble a palisade among the sea people
call in the reeds and ashes of forgiveness

your hymn
overstates the future, for this
I am punished
        the voice of river and sea meet
        swim among the salmon, answer the bark
        of river seals and winds away along the fiery curve of the world

the insouciant myth
insistent as the river's opinion
as yours, announces your presence. I am lost in fog
an apprehension caught in the spiders' web
the found wheel turning

II.
At the edge of a clearing
in the long twilight

I am with you
nestle against your warm coarse hair
you tell me
I will be safe, the fine mist begs me to believe you

but, as you may guess,
when you leave
I have only your songs
still, the fire is warm, and it's a long way until dark

III.
this is the way in which myth begins:
when the tide is close
a shadow
creases the sundown sky

        A woman
        collects fire wood from the drift spit wreckage
        along the shore,
        gold coins lie buried in her pockets
        her footprints wash away with the incoming tide.

ABOUT ALEXANDRA ELLEN APPEL:

I am very much a Poet of Place. My work reflects opposition and confrontation in a paradox of faith. My poetry follows the dictates of my heart. I use language, complex and simple, in a juxtaposition of metaphors to create an angle of thought within the richness of Place. I imagine I will write and read poetry until nothing remains. Poetry is what I do.

This 31page collection, assembled from various states of mind, reflects my lives in Idaho, California, Vermont, Alaska and Ireland.

In 1999, I earned a Doctor Degree in Education from the University of Vermont. For the degree, I authored a Philosophy of Education based on an Eco-psychologic Perspective.

Publications:

My work appears in literary journals and anthologies. Below is a short list spanning the years between 2023 and 2009:

The Freedom of New Beginnings: Poems of Witness and Vision

Poetry Crossing Press

a Taurean Horn Press Imprint, Petaluma, CA 2022

In The Light of Peace

Bayit Publishers

Williamstown, MA, 2021

WRITERS in the Attic: The Cabin, Anthology

MOON, 2022

APPLE, 2020

ANIMAL, *2016*

a Log Cabin Imprint, Boise, ID

CIRQUE, A Literary Journal for the North Pacific Rim, Anchorage, AK

Volume 26, No 1, 2023

Volume 11, No. 1, 2020

Volume 9,   No. 2, 2018

Volume 8,   No. 2, 2017

Volume 7,   No. 1, 2015

Volume 6,   No. 1, 2014

Volume 5,   No. 1, 2013

Volume 4,   No. 1, 2012

Volume 3,   No. 2, 2012

Volume 2,   No. 2, 2011

Volume 1,   No. 2, 2009

ACKNOWLEDGEMENTS:

With love and gratitude, I thank Mikki, Henry, Chance, Apollo and Adam.

Thank you, Dominic Moriarty for the gracious loan of the Rusty Gate gracing both front and back cover of this collection. It's perfect.

And, of special note, my deep felt thanks to Mark Davidson @ Hedgehog Poetry Press, for bringing this wee collection to light.